Buddhist Essays I

Five Titles

Ven. Professor Bhikkhu

Dhammavihari

Buddhist Publication Society
Kandy • Sri Lanka

Buddhist Publication Society
P.O. Box 61
54, Sangharaja Mawatha
Kandy, Sri Lanka

National Library of Sri Lanka –
Cataloguing–in–Publication Data

Bhikkhu Dhammavihari
Buddhist Essays I / Dhammavihari Bhikkhu
Kandy : Buddhist Publication Society Inc., 2002
60p.; 18cm.– (The Wheel Publication; No.446/447)

ISBN 955-24-0229–8

i.294.3 DDC 21
1. Buddhism ii. Title

ISBN 955-24-0229–8

Printed in Sri Lanka
The Quality Printers
17/2, Pangiriwatta Road
Gangodawila
Nugagoda

THE WHEEL PUBLICATION No. 446/447

Contents

1. Aesthetic Enjoyment within the Framework of Buddhist Thinking

2. Buddhism and Beauty

3. Woman within the Religious frame of Buddhism

4. The Human resource as viewed from the Buddhist Religio-cultural Angle

5. Death – Let it be thy Guide Through Life

Author's Preface

The essays in this collection have been written over a period of nearly fifty years. During the first forty years of this I was a householder. It is only at the age of sixty-nine that I took to the life of a Buddhist monk. From the age of twenty-five I have been a teacher of Buddhism and the Pali language at Universities, both here and abroad, and have handled these disciplines all my life for more than forty years.

These five essays cover four major areas. Two deal with aesthetic enjoyment and concepts of beauty as envisioned in Buddhism. As one would always discover in my writings, one may see in these two essays some elements of provocative thinking. I am fully conscious of this as I write. But I have also to be sensitive to what I read in the original texts and to come to grips with what they endeavour to communicate. I would rise up even to agree to disagree.

Next we take up the very challenging question of the position of women in Buddhism. It is known to be a subject of endless debate. Let us talk about it with a desirable academic detachment and an honest awareness of the purpose of our controversies.

Very few people know about Buddhism's concern for social growth and development. We devote one essay for the analytical and evaluative study of human resources. Why should it lie idle or be recklessly used?

Finally, we examine the reality of death in life and use it as a source of inspiration and guidance.

By the time you finish reading these essays, I cordially invite you to give me a feedback, so that I can improve the quality of my writing.

Aesthetic Enjoyment within the Framework of Buddhist Thinking

A brief study

Aesthetic sensibility and enjoyment, primarily and essentially, consist of our reactions to our environment. In the philosophy of the Buddha we discover a wealth of information which helps us to plan and adjust our life in the world in a healthy, reasonable and justifiable way. Through this philosophy, we get out of our life in the world the maximum benefit and happiness. We also do not allow ourselves to tread on others' corns or, unwittingly though, burn our own fingers. This, it must be remembered, is a fundamental concept of our *dharma* or the Buddhist norm. It is the rule of *attūpanāyika*, i.e. that one acts and reacts towards others in the same way that one likes to be treated by others (e.g. *attānaṃ upamaṃ katvā na haneyya na ghātaye.* Dhp.v.129).

It is the recurrent theme of the Ambalaṭṭhikā Rāhulovāda Sutta of the Majjhima Nikāya (MN.I. 414 ff.), where the Buddha admonishes his son Rāhula that before doing anything through thought, word or deed, one should scrutinize carefully (*paccavekkhitvā paccavekkhitvā kattabbaṃ)* whether such action stands to the detriment of oneself (*attavyābādhāya)* or to the detriment of others (*paravyābādhāya).* In evolving such a sensible and rewarding philosophy of life, the Buddhists do not withdraw into a frozen ice-chamber or plunge into an arid dry desert. Nor do they have to, with an unwarranted idea of the holy, set the spirit to fight against the body and practise severe asceticism.

Therefore this does not necessarily carry with it the renunciation complexion generally associated with the shaven-headed, dyed-robed monk. Nevertheless, it would ultimately lead to the highest achievements of Buddhist religious living which both converge in and are gathered at the perfect state of ego-lessness required of the recluse, often described as a state of dignified detachment.

The philosophy of the Buddha and the way of life he recommended was in marked contrast to what was prevalent in certain circles in India at the time. In the religious controversies of the time, in the battle of the spirit against the body, the flesh was tortured and human life was degraded to lamentably low depths. These are described in graphic detail in the Mahāsaccaka Sutta of the Majjhima Nikāya (MN.1. 242-5) where the Bodhisatta, while he was yet experimenting in his search for release, is seen indulging in them. Finally the Bodhisatta rejected them as being of no avail. Once King Pasenadi of Kosala, while he was in the company of the Buddha, spoke of the followers of such creeds in the following words:

"There I see recluses and Brahmins who are emaciated and lean, discoloured and looking exceedingly pale. The veins have become visible all over their bodies. People will indeed not be delighted to see them." (See MN II.121. Dhammacetiya Sutta).

When these religious men were questioned by the King as to what motivated them into these austere practices, their reply was that it was their religious heritage and that this self-inflicted physical tyranny was part of their religious discipline (*Bandhuka-rogo no mahārājā'ti.* loc.cit). Religious men who indulged in such practices freely roamed the streets of India then as some of them do even today.

In the above description of some of the contemporary Indian ascetics as being repulsive, the original texts use a phrase which means 'do not catch the eye of the onlooker' (*Na viya maññe cakkhuṃ bandhanti janassa dassanāya*). This means that on seeing them, feelings of pleasure or joy do not arise in the minds of people. We call an object which comes within the range of our vision beautiful, under normal conditions, in relation to the degree of pleasurable feelings it generates within us, i.e. to the degree of pleasurable acceptability we are willing to offer it. In this realm of beauty, namely visual, colour and form are dominant considerations. In defining or judging beauty, whether there are absolute criteria in relation to colour and form, is a debatable point. They are judged, for the most part, on accepted values, accepted collectively or individually. Through collective persuasion, impersonally though, these values acquire semi-absolute standards.

Groups, as much as individuals, would declare things as being beautiful on this basis. If one were to thoroughly simplify this concept of beauty, one could say 'a thing of beauty is joy for ever'. Likewise objects also become capable of giving delight and producing pleasurable feelings through personal association. Such objects then become beautiful, meaningful and significant. Here, memory as well as personal identification and association as well as re-creation and re-association of situations of the past sometimes add to the beauty of an object of the present.

Although this appears to be a totally subjective approach and hence bound to lead to a diversity of notions and standards, one can nevertheless discern at times an objective continuity running through this diversity. In these cases we are looking at the beauty-value of objects from the point of their producing pleasurable feelings in the minds of those who behold them. At the same time, beauty does not need to be always equivalent to what is pretty or good-looking, as expressed in common parlance.

Objects which are not pretty on the normally accepted terms are capable of stimulating emotions and giving aesthetic delight because of their special significance to the person concerned. Here, it is not the mere subjective, personal factor. One uses here a different yard-stick, out of the common run of man. In defining beauty

and and the appeal of beauty, this is what is sometimes called 'the action of the mind.' Even what is weird and grotesque, is capable at times of being beautiful and producing aesthetic delight. The disciples of the Buddha, with their serene sense of detachment, found such places and things particularly inspiring. The venerable Sariputta, undoubtedly the foremost of the Buddha's disciples, is found commending in the verses of the Theragāthā, the austerity of the dwelling place of his younger brother, Revata. Thus he says:

In village or the wild, in vale or hill,
Wherever the men of worth, the arahants
Their dwelling make, delightful is the spot.
Delightful are the forests, where no crowd
Doth come to take its pleasures; there will they
Who are released from passions find their joy.
Not seekers they for sense-satiety.

(Thag. *vv*. 991-2)

Note here the words 'Not seekers they for sense-satiety' (*na te kāma-gavesino).* For evidently, a good part of true beauty would indeed be shut out from those who are mere pleasure-seekers. Elsewhere in the Theragāthā, the sylvan retreats which Kassapa the Great describes as soul-delighting, had indeed a beauty which was peculiarly their own:

Those upland glades delightful to the soul,
Where the Kareri spreads its wildering wreaths,
Where sound the trumpet-calls of elephant:
Those are the braes wherein my soul delights.
Those rocky heights with hue of dark blue clouds,
Where lies enbosomed many a shining tarn
Of crystal-clear, cool waters and whose slopes
The 'herds of Indra' cover and bedeck:
Those are the braes wherein my soul delights.

Like serried battlements of blue-black cloud
Like pinnacles on stately castle built,
Re-echoing to the cries of jungle folk:
Those are the braes wherein my soul delights.

Thag. *vv.*1062-64

Crags where clear waters lie, a rocky world,
Haunted by black-faced apes and timid deer,
Carpeted with watery moss and lichen:
Those are the braes wherein my soul delights.

Thag. *v.* 1070

In the above verses, expressions like 'Where sound the trumpet-calls of elephants', 'Re-echoing to the cries of jungle folk', 'Haunted by black-faced apes and timid deer' and 'Carpeted with watery moss and lichen' have a distinctness of their own. It must also be conceded that they reflect the emergence of a particular culture pattern. But the extent to which it found expression and developed later to a fuller richness, depended on the particular genius of the different people into whose midst Buddhism found its way. Buddhists of Japan, particularly those of the early Zen tradition stand unique in this respect.

To give our listeners a sampling of the heights to which Buddhist thinking elevated Japanese poets, let me quote a couple of verses written by the great Haiku poet of Japan of the 17th century - Master Basho. Sitting lonely in a solitary hut with only a banana plant nearby as his good neighbour, Basho writes -

A banana plant in the autumn gale -
I listen to the dripping of rain
Into a basin at night.

Does this not remind one of the ecstasies of the forest-dwelling monks of the Theragāthā we have discussed in detail above? Here is yet another from Master Basho and his comrade poets:

Above a town
Filled with the odours of things,
The Summer moon.
" It's hot! It's hot ! "
Murmurs are heard in the front yards.

What a beautiful study in contrast of our bustling metropolitan life which we ourselves have created and the potential of inner peace which lies so close with nature in the world outside! As man of mature sanctity and deep conviction, a fortnight before his death Basho wrote this haiku:

A white chrysanthemum -
However intently I gaze,
Not a speck of dirt.

This attitude also made it possible at times to convert even what was perilous and imminently dangerous into a source of delight and inspiration and to view it with admiration. Here is Thera Tālapuṭa telling us of a phase of life he has been through:

There in the jungle ringing with cries of peacock
 and of heron wilt thou dwell,
By panthers and by tigers owned as chief.
And for thy body cast off care;
Miss not thine hour, thine aim!

Thag. *v.* 1113

We run into an even more interesting situation in the story of Ekavihāriya Thera who tells us thus:

Yea, swiftly and alone, bound to my quest,
I'll to the jungle that I love, the haunt
Of infuriated elephants, the source and means
Of thrilling zest to each ascetic soul.

Thag. *v*. 539

Even an underlying threat to life like the panthers and tigers and the infuriated elephants does not appear to rob the collective ensemble of its inherent beauty. To appreciate fully the reward of this cultivated Buddhist attitude, we should particularly mark the words 'swiftly' and 'alone', 'bound to my quest', 'infuriated elephants' and 'thrilling zest to each ascetic soul'. What is of further interest to us is that the Commentary tells us that this Ekavihāriya Thera is none other than the younger brother Tissa of the Emperor Asoka.

We are told that the prince, while hunting, was so impressed at the sight of the Greek Thera Yonaka Mahā Dhammarakkhita seated under a tree, that he also longed to live so in the forest. Longing for the happiness of the recluse, he is said to have uttered the above verses. If we give adequate credence here to the Commentarial tradition, it implies the vibrant continuance of the Buddhist aesthetic values we have discussed above and their survival even after several centuries.

(All translations of the Theragāthā are from Mrs. Rhys Davids' Psalms of the Brethren).

Buddhism and Beauty

With the doctrine of *tilakkhaṇa* or *anicca, dukkha and anatta*, i.e. impermanence, unsatisfactoriness and selflessness in the forefront, is it possible to speak of a concept of beauty in Buddhism? Has it not often been suggested that Buddhism is a religion of pessimism and that with its doctrine of renunciation, Buddhism would have very little to do with notions of beauty? Although these remarks may at first appear to be very convincing, they are in fact far from the truth and are no more than mistaken generalisations. Let us first examine the doctrine of the three aforesaid characteristics or signata of existence (impermanence, unsatisfactoriness and selflessness). This, the Buddha taught his first five disciples and is recorded in the Anattalakkhaṇa Sutta (Vin.I.p.13-14) as follows:

"This body of ours (*rūpa*), O Bhikkhus, is not the self (*attā*). If the body, O Bhikkhus, were the self, the body would not be subject to disease and we should be able to say: "Let my body be such and such a one, let my body not be such and such a one."

"But since this body, O Bhikkhus, is not the self, therefore the body is subject to disease, and we are not able to say "Let my body be such and such a one, let my body not be such and such a one." And he further said: "Now what do you think, O Bhikkhus, is this body of ours permanent or perishable?" "It is perishable, Lord." "And that which is perishable, does that cause pain or joy?" "It causes pain, Lord" "And that which is perishable, painful, subject to change, is it possible to regard that in this way: "This is mine, this am I, this is my self?" "That is impossible, Lord."

In this manner the Buddha admitted the presence of unsatisfactoriness or suffering in the world, and by a method of analysis he pointed out to his disciples that attachment to things, without a correct view as to their true nature, was the cause of this suffering. Impermanence and change are inherent in the nature of all things. This is their true nature and to know it as such is the correct view, and as long as we are at variance with it, we are bound to run into conflicts. We cannot alter or control the nature of things. If we attempted to do so, the result then would be "Hope deferred maketh the heart sick." The only solution to this lies in correcting our own point of view.

The Buddha has declared that the thirst for things, no matter what they are, begets sorrow: *taṇhāya jāyati soko*. When we like persons or things, we wish that they belonged to us and were with us for ever. Consciously or unconsciously, we wish for permanency of possession. We do not stop to think about their true nature or in our great enthusiasm refuse to think about their true nature. We do not wish to entertain in our minds such concepts like loss, separation and destruction. We expect things and persons to survive time. But time devours everything (*kālo ghasati bhūtāni*). Youth must yield to old age and the freshness of the morning dew disappears before the rising sun. Both are expressions of the natural law of change.

When the Buddha lay in his death-bed at Kusinārā, his disciple and close attendant Ananda, who had not yet gained true insight and become an arahant, was unable to bear the grief on hearing about the imminent death of his master. So the Buddha, in his admonition to weeping Ananda, whom he had promptly summoned, said: "Grieve not, O Ananda, lament not. Have I not already told you that from all good things we love and cherish we would be separated, sooner or later. That they would change their nature and perish in their own way. How then can the Tathāgata not pass away? That is not possible." (DN.II.118).

This is the philosophy which underlies the doctrine of *tilakkhaṇa* or the Buddhist view of life and the world. All Buddhist values are based on this. The Buddha expected of his disciples, both laity and clergy, good conduct and good behaviour and decent standards of living in every way. He never lost sight of the fact that they had a part to play in both religion and society. With him, plain living did not amount to degenerate human existence. Dhammacetiya Sutta of the Majjhima Nikāya (MN.II.118 ff.) clearly expresses what the saner men of good judgement thought of ascetic life as it was practised in India at the time. Thus said Pasenadī of Kosala: "There I see recluses and Brahmins become emaciated and lean, discoloured and looking very pale. The veins have become visible all over the body. People will not be delighted to see them, I fear." In the Pāli original of this, there is a phrase which is of interest to us: *na viya maññe cakkhuṃ bandhanti janassa dassanāya.* (Ibid. 121). This means that they do not catch the eye of the onlooker.

Here, we have one definite notion of beauty. An object of beauty is something which we are pleased to see. Hence, we get the term *pāsādika* (pleasant or pleasing) used over and over again with reference to the dress and demeanour of the Buddhist monk. Of personal cleanliness, decency and decorum, the Buddha spoke in praise, not only for their own sake but also because of their social implications. Among the regulations governing the monastic life in Buddhism there are many instructions which bear testimony to this. Healthy living has been the *sine qua non* of Buddhism - *ārogyā paramā lābhā* (Dhp. *v.* 204) or freedom from disease, the Buddha said, is the greatest gain.

This attitude, in addition to safeguarding the general health of a people, also resulted in creating an environment which is aesthetically pleasing. And the following passage from the Mahāvagga of the Vinayapiṭaka clearly illustrates that the simple life which the Buddha advocated was not without standards.

"If there are cobwebs in the *vihāra* or the place of residence, let him remove them as soon as he sees them. Let him wipe off the casements and corners of the room. If a wall which is coated with red chalk is dirty, let him moisten the mop, wring it out, and scour the wall. If the floor is coated black and is dirty, let him moisten the mop, wring it out, and scour the floor. If the floor is not black-

ened let him sprinkle it with water and scrub it in order that the *vihāra* may not become dusty. Let him heap up the sweepings and cast them aside. Let him bask the carpet in the sun, clean it, dust it by beating, take it back, and spread it out as it was spread before" (Vin.I.48).

Thus we see that the Buddha was no ascetic who attempted to elevate the soul by resorting to forms of conduct which are repulsive and debasing. But beauty, the Buddha maintained, if one does not understand the true nature of objects of beauty, may lead to grief and disappointment. It distorts values and upsets the standards of judgement. When beauty is limited to persons and things, greed and pride are the lot of those who possess them. If such things are not common and are not easily obtained, a man may be called upon to engage himself in an eternal struggle to safeguard his exclusive possessions. On the other hand, those who have set unlimited values on their coveted objects of beauty but are not fortunate enough to possess them, will need great strength and courage to resist their feelings of jealousy and enmity towards those who have the good fortune to possess them.

Here we are reminded of the story of Venerable Pakkha in the

Theragāthā (Thag.*v*.63). One day, going to the village for alms, he sat down beneath a tree. Then a kite, seizing some flesh flew up into the sky. Him, many kites attacked, making him drop the meat. Another kite grabbed the fallen flesh, and was plundered by yet another. And the bhikkhu thought to himself: "Just like that meat are worldly desires, common to all, full of pain and woe."And reflecting thereon, and realizing how they were impermanent he resolved to carry out his mission in full. He sat down for his afternoon rest, and expanding insight won arahantship.

It becomes clearly evident from these that the Buddhist does not avoid objects of beauty nor does he run away from them. He only refrains from making them the basis for strong and individuated likes and dislikes. Whatever there is in the world, pleasant and lovable, we are attached to them, and we develop a dislike towards their opposites. Placed in this philosophical setting, the Buddhist recognizes beauty where the senses can perceive it. But in beauty he also sees its own change and destruction. He remembers what the Buddha said with regard to all component things, that they come into being, undergo change and are destroyed.

Therefore the wise man acquires a greater depth of vision. His admiration is not coloured by a greed for acquisition and possession. This is exactly the message imparted where the Buddha says "Whatever beautiful things there are in the world, they are not, in themselves. lustful things (*kāmā)*. It is the greedy thoughts of man (*saṅkapparāgo*) which makes them lustful. The beautiful things in the world remain as they are, while the wise men restrain their desires."

Na te kāmā yāni citrāni loke
saṃkapparāgo purisassa kāmo
tiṭṭhanti citrāni tath' eva loke
ath'ettha dhīrā vinayanti chandaṃ.

SN. I. 22

The disciples of the Buddha understood this and proved it in their own lives. There was Venerable Sappaka, who taking from the Buddha an exercise for spiritual culture, went to the Lonagiri Vihāra on the banks of the river Ajakaraṇī. There was beauty all around him and the peace of the place seems to have satisfied him so much that after his enlightenment he decided to make it his permanent abode. We see his heart filled with joy as he describes the beauty of the place. But note what a remarkable sense of detachment he yet displays.

When I see the crane, her clear bright wings
Outstretched in fear to flee the black storm cloud,
A shelter seeking, to safe shelter borne,
Then doth the river Ajakaraṇī give joy to me.

Who doth not love to see on either bank
Clustered rose apple trees in fairy array
Behind the great cave of my hermitage
Or here the soft croak of the frogs, well rid
Of their undying mortal foes proclaim:
Not from the mountain streams isn't time today
To flit. Safe is the Ajakaraṇī.
She brings us luck. Here is it good to be.

(Thag.*vv*.307-310).

In the enjoyment of beauty Sappaka is not agitated. What needs ruffle him and disturb his peace? There is nothing that he is in danger of losing and nothing that he needs to posses and jealously guard. Herein the mind is freed from pettiness and strife, and therein man finds contentment and rest. Kassapa, the Great, reiterates the same with great conviction when he says:

Those upland glades delightful to the soul
Where the Kareri spreads its wildering wreaths,
Where sound the trumpet-calls of elephants:
Those are the braes wherein my soul delights.
Those rocky heights with hue of dark blue clouds,
Where lies embosomed many a shining tarn
Of crystal clear, cool waters. and where slopes
The "herds of Indra" cover and bedeck:
Here is enough for me who fain would dwell
In meditation rapt, mindful and tense.

Thag. *vv*. 1067f .

And as we have already stated earlier, the Buddhist does not build a wall around himself to shut out the world of sense experience. He remains within it. Does not Thera Kāludāyi who describes the beauty of the season speak like a poet or an artist?

Now crimson glow the trees, dear Lord, and cast
Their ancient foliage in quest of fruit.
Like crests of flame they shine irradiant,
And rich in hope, great Hero, is the hour.
Verdure and blossom-time in every tree,
Where we look delightful to the eye,
And every quarter breathing fragrant airs,
While petals falling, yearning comes for fruit.

(Thag. *vv*. 527f).

In him, it is not a mere passive eye that only records what is seen which is at work but also a heart that responds and reacts. But our Thera Kāludāyi does so with understanding and judgement. And this philosophical attitude of the Buddhist to beauty may best be summed up in the following words of the Japanese poet who sang:

"On Mount Yoshino each returning year,
How beautiful the cherries blossom gay.
Split the tree open wide and then draw near,
Tell me where is the flower now, I pray."

This is the philosophy of change and continuity. And in it, fail not to see beauty which can ever be to man an unending source of inspiring joy.

Woman Within the Religious Frame of Buddhism

At the time the Buddha set up his Order of Bhikkhus, there was in Indian society the widespread but groundless belief that woman is inferior to man. The position which the woman lost under the dominance of the Brahmanas had not yet been retrieved. The brahmins of the day evidently showed little sympathy for her sad lot. Altekar describes the position of women in India at the time as follows: "The prohibition of *upanayana* amounted to spiritual disenfranchisement of women and produced a disastrous effect upon their general position in society. It reduced them to the status of Sudras... What, however, did infinite harm to women was the theory that they were ineligible for them (Vedic sacrifices) because they were of the status of the Sudras."

Henceforward they began to be bracketed with éudras and other backward classes in society. This we find to be the case even in the Bhagavadgītā IX.32, (Altekar, A.S.The Position of Women in Hindu Civilization, pp.204f.). In the Manusmṛti we witness the cruel infliction of domestic subservience on women. The road to heaven is barred to her and there is hard bargaining with her for the offer of an alternative route. Matrimony and obedience to the husband are the only means whereby a woman can hope to reach heaven.

Nāsti strīnāṃ pṛthag yajño na vrataṃ nāpyupoṣathaṃ
patiṃ susrūṣate yena tena svarge mahīyate.

(Manu. V.153).

"Women have no sacrifices of their own to perform
Nor religious rites or observances to follow.
Obedience to the husband alone would exalt the woman in heaven."

This hostile attitude to women both in religion and in society was repeatedly criticised and challenged by the Buddha on numerous occasions. In the Kosala Saṃyutta (SN. I. 86) the Buddha contradicts the belief that the birth of a daughter was not as much a cause of joy as that of a son, a belief which the ritualism of the Brahmanas had contributed to strengthen. The Buddha pointed out clearly that the woman had a dignified and an important part to play in society, and he defined it with great insight, fitting her harmoniously into the social fabric. She is a lovable member of the household, held in place by numerous relationships, and respected above all, as the mother of worthy sons. The sex did not matter, he argued, and added that in character and in her role in society, she may even rival men:

Itthī pi hi ekacciyā seyyā posā janādhipa
medhāvinī sīlavatī sassudevā patibbatā.
Tassā yo jāyati poso sūro hoti disampati
evam subhagiyā putto rajjam pi anusāsati.

SN. I,86

"A woman child, O lord of men, may prove
Even a better offspring than a male.
For she may grow up wise and virtuous,
Her husband's mother reverencing, true wife.
The boy that she may bear may do great deeds,
And rule great realms, yea, such a son
Of noble wife becomes his country's guide."

(Kindred Sayings I,p.111).

But it is not unusual to find scholars who have missed this singular virtue of Buddhism. It would be grossly unfair to say that the Buddha did not devote much attention to the duties and ideals of lay women or that he showed indifference to or contempt of women. Speaking of Buddhism and Jainism Altekar unjustly says: "Both these were ascetic religions, and they have not devoted much attention to the duties and ideals of lay women. The founders and leaders of both these novements showed the indifference to, or contempt of women, which is almost universal among the advocates of the ascetic ideal." (Altekar, A.S., op.cit. p.208).

The instances are numerous where the Buddha defines and describes the duties of women in society (AN.IV, 265f). Further, the Buddha recognises the fact that these do not constitute the whole of their life. It is not with a view to limiting their life solely to the secular affairs of the household that the Buddha laid down a code of good living for women, but to serve as a complement to the good life already enjoined in his religion to all his followers, irrespective of their sex. A host of these considerations as they are addressed to women are grouped together in the Saṃyutta Nikāya in a chapter solely devoted to them (SN.IV,328f). A good lay woman endowed with religious devotion, moral virtue and liberality as well as wisdom and learning, makes a success of her life in this world. For it is said:

Saddhāya sīlena ca yīdha vaḍḍhati
paññāya cāgena sutena cābhayam
sā tādisī sīlavatī upāsikā ādiyati
sāraṃ idheva attano ti.

(SN. IV.250).

"Such a virtuous lady who possesses religious devotion,
Cultivates virtue, is endowed with wisdom and learning
And is given to charity makes a success of her life in this very existence."

Her virtuous character gives to her life in the household poise and dignity: *Pañcahi bhikkhave dhammehi samannāgato mātugāmo visārado agāram ajjhāvasati. Katamehi pañcahi? Pāṇātipātā paṭivirato ca hoti... surāmeraya-majjapamādaṭṭhānā paṭivirato ca hoti.* (SN.IV, 250.). The following are also given as virtues by means of which she can make her life fruitful, both here and hereafter: *Saddho* (religious devotion), *hirimā ottappī* (sense of shame and fear), *akkodhano anupanāhī* (not given to anger), *anissukī* (not jealous), *amaccharī* (not niggardly), *anaticārī* (chaste in behaviour), *sīlavā* (virtuous), *bahussuto* (learned), *āraddhaviriyo* (zealous), *upaṭṭhitassati* (mentally alert), *paññavā* (wise). Ibid.243-44.

We notice that all these virtues enumerated so far are within the reach of a woman living in the household. She is not rooted out of her domestic setting. The good and successful life of the laywoman, as much as of the layman, seems to have loomed large in the ethics of Buddhism. In the Anguttara Nikāya, two sets of virtues are given whereby a woman is said to strive for success in this world as well as in the other - *idhalokavijaya* and *paralokavijaya* (*Catūhi kho Visākha dhammehi samannāgato mātugāmo idhalokavijayāya patipanno hoti ayam sa loko āraddho hoti. Katamehi catūhi? Idha Visākha mātugāmo susamvihita-kammanto hoti sangahitaparijano bhattu manāpam carati sambhatam anurakkhati... Catūhi kho Visākha dhammehi samannāgato mātugāmo paralokavijāyaya patipanno hoti parassa loko araddho hoti. Katamehi catūhi? Idha Visākha mātugāmo saddhāsampanno hoti sīlasampanno hoti cāgasampanno hoti paññāsampanno hoti*- AN. IV, 269f.).

It is also worth noting here that the Buddha accepts the reality and significance of the instituton of marriage for women. But, unlike in Hindu society, it was not the only means for the social elevation of women. In Hinduism, a woman is supposed to become a *dvija*, a truly initiated member of the religion and the society, only after her marriage (Prabhu, *Hindu Social Organisatio*, p.284).

The virtues referred to in the Anguttara Nikāya (AN.IV,269f.) are household duties of a woman as wife which lead to domestic peace and concord. They are also calculated to keep the family administration in gear and secure for the family economic stability. This significant part which she is called upon to play is meticulously defined and it reveals neither indifference to nor contempt of women on the part of the Buddha.

The good laywoman has also her duties for the development of her religious life. It is a course of graduated training which does not conflict with her household life. It is, in fact, smoothly woven into it. Religious devotion (*saddhā*), moral virtue (*sīla*), and a generous disposition (*cāga*), for instance, form part of it. This healthy combination of social and religious virtues of a woman is further witnessed in the Anguttaṛa Nikāya where it is said that the following eight virtues pave the way for her to proceed to heaven:

Susamvihitakammantā sangahitaparijjanā
bhattu manāpaṃ carati sambhatam anurakkhati.
Saddhāsīlena sampannā vadaññū vītamaccharā
niccaṃ maggaṃ visodheti sotthānaṃ samparāyikaṃ.
Iccete aṭṭhadhammā ca yassa vijjati nāriyā
tam pi sīlavatim āhu dhammaṭṭhaṃ saccavādinim.
Solasākārasampannā aṭṭhaṅgasusamāgatā
tādisī sīlavatī upāsikā upapajjati devalokaṃ manāpaṃ.

(AN.IV,271).

They are:
1. organises the work of the household with efficiency,
2. treats her servants with concern,
3. strives to please her husband,
4. takes good care of what he earns,
5. possesses religious devotion,
6. is virtuous in conduct,
7. is kind,
8. is liberal.

The first four items of this list are identical with the first four of the five good qualities ascribed to the virtuous wife in the Sigālovāda Sutta, the fifth being general efficiency (*dakkhā*) and enterprise (*analasā sabbakiccesu*): DN.III,190.

It was also held in Indian belief that woman was intellectually inferior to man and therefore had no capacity to reach higher spiritual attainments. This idea clearly echoes in the Saṃyutta Nikāya where Māra, as the personification of the forces of evil, strives in vain to dissuade a bhikkhunī from her religious endeavours:

> *Yaṃ taṃ isīhi pattabbaṃ ṭhānaṃ durabhisambhavaṃ*
> *na taṃ dvaṅgulapaññāya sakkā pappotuṃ itthiyā.*

(SN.I,129).

> "No woman, with the two-finger-wisdom which is hers,
> could ever hope to reach those heights which are attained
> only by the sages."

These words of Māra are undoubtedly resonant of the beliefs of the day and the Buddha was vehement in contradicting them. Bhikkhunī Somā to whom Māra addressed these words answered, illustrating the Buddhist attitude to the spiritual potentialities of women:

Itthibhāvo no kiṃ kayirā cittamhi susamāhite
ñānamhi vattamānamhi sammā dhammaṃ vipassato.

Ibid.

"When one's mind is well-concentrated and
wisdom never fails
does the fact of our being women make any
difference?"

However, there is evidence that this age-old scepticism about the spiritual potentialities of women died hard. Even in the face of success achieved by bhikkhunīs in Buddhism, a groundless belief seems to have prevailed which distrusted the capacity of women for spiritual perfection. On the eve of her final passing away, when Mahāpajāpatī Gotamī visits the Buddha to bid him farewell, he calls upon her to give proof of the religious attainments of the bhikkhunīs in order to convince the disbelieving sceptics, the men in society:

Thīnaṃ dhammābhisamaye ye bālā vimatiṃ gatā
tesaṃ diṭṭhipahānattham iddhim dassehi Gotamī.

Apadān, II,.535.

"O Gotami, perform a miracle in order to dispel the wrong views of those foolish men who are in doubt with regard to the spiritual potentialities of women."

Buddhism, with its characteristic note of realism, also recognises the inherent qualities of women which make them attractive to the opposite sex. Nothing else in the world, it is said, can delight and cheer a man so much as a woman. In her, one would find all the fivefold pleasures of the senses. The world of pleasure exists in her.

Pañcakāmaguṇā ete itthirūpasmiṃ dissare
rūpā saddā rasā gandhā phoṭṭhabbā ca manoramā.

AN.III, 69.

"All these five-fold pleasures of the senses which gratify the mind are centered in the feminine form."

The power which the woman derives through this may, at the same time, extend so far as to make man throw all reason to the winds and be a pawn in her hand, under the influence of her charm. Thus, it is even possible that a mother may err in relation to her son or *vice versa.*

Kin nu so bhikkhave moghapuriso maññati na mātā putte sārajjati putto vā pana mātari ti. (Ibid. 68).

"What, O monks, does that foolish man think that a mother would not feel lustfully attached to her son or the son to his mother?" See Gradual Sayings, III,p.55 for a different translation of this passage which we consider to be incorrect.

Therefore a man might say without exaggeration that woman is a trap laid out on all sides by Māra (*Yaṃ hi taṃ bhikkhave sammā vadamāno vadeyya samantapāso mārassā ti mātugāmaṃ yeva sammā vadamāno vadeyya samantapāso mārassā ti* - ibid). These observations are made, however, not as a stricture on their character but as a warning to men, who in seeking their company, might err on the side of excess. It is true that at times they tend to be overstressed, but obviously with no malice to women. There is pointed reference to the unguarded nature of the man who falls a prey to these feminine charms.

Muṭṭhassatiṃ tā bandhanti pekkhitena mihitena ca
atho pi dunnivatthena mañjunā bhaṇitena ca
neso jano svāsaddo api ugghātito mato.

(AN. III,69).

"Women ensnare a man of heedless mind with their glances and smiles or with artful grooming (*dunnivattha* = inadequately clad) and pleasing words. Women are such that one cannot approach them in safety even though they may be stricken and dead" (G.S.III,57).

Thus it becomes clear that it is not in the spirit of Buddhism to brand women as a source of corruption for man. Note the words 'a man of heedless mind' in the above quotation. It would be interesting to contrast here the words of Manu who says, 'It is the nature of women to seduce men in this world': *Svabhāva eva nārīnāṃ narānāṃ iha dūṣaṇaṃ* - (Manu.II,213). The Jains too, in spite of their admission of women into the Monastic Order, do not seem to have differed very much from the Brahmins in their attitude towards women. The Ācāraṅga Sūtra, in the course of a religious admonition known as the Pillow of Righteousness, makes the following comment which stigmatises women completely: 'He to whom women were known as the causes of all sinful acts, he saw the true state of the world.' (Jaina Sūtras I, SBE. XXII,p.81).

The position of women in Jainism is summed up as follows: "Right in the earliest portions of the Canon a woman is looked upon as something evil that enticed innocent males into a snare of misery. They are described as 'the greatest temptation', 'the causes of all sinful acts'. 'the slough', 'demons' etc. Their bad qualities are described in exaggerated terms. Their passions are said to destroy the celibacy of monks 'like a pot filled with lac near fire' ". (Deo.S.B., *History of Jaina Monachism*, p.493). In Buddhism, on the other hand, the caution which men are called upon to exercise in their dealings with the opposite sex springs solely from the Buddhist attitude to *kāma* or the pleasures of the senses. *Kāma* are described in Buddhism as leading to grief and turbulence. *Kāma* thwart the path to transcendental happiness. This attitude is eloquently manifest in the counsel given to Ariṭṭha in the Alagaddūpama Sutta (MN. I,130).

Of this vast field of sense experience of man, sex is only a segment but it is admittedly one with irresistible appeal and thus required a special word of warning, particularly to those who are keen on the pursuit of mental equipoise. The Buddha says that if it were left unbridled, it would, in expressing itself, shatter all bounds of propriety (*Kin nu so bhikkhave moghapuriso maññati na mātā putte sārajjati putto vā pana mātarī ti;* AN. III,68. Already quoted above).

Hence the desire to lead a chaste and moral life, eschewing, even completely, the gratification of sex desires, can as much be the aspiration of a woman as that of a man. Besides this philosophic attitude to the pleasures of the world in which the woman admittedly plays a dominant part, there seems to be nothing in Buddhism which looks upon sex or woman as being corrupt in themselves.

Thus it becomes clear that the philosophy of early Buddhism had no reservations whatsoever regarding the spiritual emancipation of women. In the ocean of *saṃsāra* her chances of swimming across to the farther shore were as good as those of man. Emancipation of the mind through perfection of wisdom, which is referred to as *cetovimutti: paññāvimutti* was the goal of religious life and for this the way which had proved most effective was the life of renunciation. The woman was as much encumbered by household life as man and in her spiritual earnestness she would have equally well echoed the words of the man who chooses renunciation. She would say with him that the household life is full of impediments and contrast it with the life of *pabbajjā* (*Sambādho gharāvāso rajopatho abbhokāso pabbajjā*: MN.I,179).

But according to the evidence of the Pali texts (AN.IV,274 & Vin.II,253) the admission of women into the life of *pabbajjā* in Buddhism does not seem to have been effected with as much ease as one would expect. According to these, the Buddha appears to have shown some reluctance to admit women into the Order. When Mahāpajāpatī Gotamī requested the Buddha to consent to the entry of women into his Order he is said to have put her off three times, saying: 'Do not be interested O, Gotamī, about the entry of women into my Order' (ibid). This does seem to imply that the presence of women in the monastic institution of *brahmacariya* was considered, for some reason or other, to be detrimental to its well-being. In an atmosphere where women were considered a danger to spiritual life, their presence in the inner circle of religious life as members of the monastic community would have naturally called for serious comment.

However, there is evidence that Jainism had already broken through this barrier against women. But the vicissitudes of the Jaina monastic community, in its relations between the two orders of monks and nuns, as well as of nuns and laymen, could not apparently have been very heartening to the Buddha. Speaking of the reforms introduced by Mahāvīra with the addition of the fifth vow of chastity to the earlier *catuyāma saṃvara* of Pārsva, Jacobi says, 'The argumentation in the text presupposes a decay of morals of the monastic order to have occurred between Pārsva and Mahāvīra.' (Jaina Sūtras, II, SBE.XLV,122 n.3). There is also evidence from another quarter of the promiscuity in the behaviour of male and female mendicants in the Buddha's day. The Buddha takes note of this in the Culladhammasamādāna Sutta.

He speaks of Samaṇas and Brāhmaṇas who repudiating the view that sensual pleasures are detrimental to spiritual progress, mingle freely with female mendicants, vociferously enjoying their company. They are reported as saying: 'Whatever can be the basis for pleading for the renunciation of sensual pleasures? What future calamity can lie in wait for us? Blissful indeed is the contact of the soft and tender hands of these young female mendicants' (MN.I,305).

However, the Buddha concedes to Ānanda that women, having

taken to the life of *pabbajjā* in Buddhism, are capable of attaining the higher fruits of religious life as far as Arahantship. (*Bhabbo Ānanda, mātugamo tathāgatappavedite dhammavinaye agarasmā anagāriyaṃ pabbajitvā sotāpattiphalaṃ pi sakadāgāmiphalaṃ pi anāgāmiphalaṃ pi arahattaphalaṃ pi sacchikātun'ti.* AN.IV,276 & Vin.II, 254). The considerations which seem to have weighed heavy in the mind of the Buddha regarding the admission of women into the Order are concerned more with the wider problem of the monastic organization as a whole. He would have been undoubtedly most averse to stand in the way of the personal liberty of women. But in the interests of the collective good of the institution of *brahmacariya*, which was the core of the religion, women had to make certain sacrifices, surrendering at times even what might appear to have been their legitimate rights. This is evident from the following eight conditions (*aṭṭhagarudhammā)* under which the Buddha granted them permission to enter the Order:

1. A nun who has been ordained (even) for a hundred years must greet respectfully, rise up from her seat, salute with joined palms, do proper homage to a monk ordained but that day.

2. A nun must not spend the rains in a residence where there are no monks.(See Bhikkhunī Pāc.56: Vin.IV,313).

3. Every halfmonth a nun should desire two things from the Order of monks: the asking (as to the date) of the Observance day, and the coming for the exhortation. (See Bhikkhunī Pāc.59: Vin.315).

4. After the rains a nun must 'invite' before both Orders in respct of three matters: what was seen, what was heard, what was suspected. (See Bhikkhuni Pac. 57: Vin. 314.)

5. A nun, offending against an important rule, must undergo

mānatta (discipline) for half a month before both Orders.

6. When, as a probationer, she has trained in the six rules for two years, she should seek higher ordination from both Orders.

7. A Monk must not be abused or reviled in any way by a nun.

8. From today admonition of monks by nuns is forbidden, admonition of nuns by monks is not forbidden. (*Book of the Discipline*, V,354-55).

The insistence on these *aṭṭhagarudhammā* is the most vital issue, much more than the delayed consent of the Buddha, in the founding of the Bhikkhunī Sāsana. The delay, it may in fact be argued, would have proved useful to emphasise the conditions which he was going to lay down. It is these conditions alone which gave the women access to the monastic life in Buddhism (*Sace Ānanda Mahāpajāpatī Gotamī aṭṭhagarudhamme paṭigaṇhāti sā va'ssa hotu upasampadā*: Vin.II,255). The Dharmagupta Vinaya in the Chinese version compares them to a bridge over a great river by means of which one is enabled to cross over to the farther bank (*Taisho*, Vol.22,p.923 B). These *garudhammā* are observances which pertain to monastic propriety and procedure in the Order of Bhikkhunīs in relation to the Bhikkhus. The women are not to violate these as long as they remain in the monastic community.

In the establishment of the Bhikkhunī Sāsana, these conditions seem to have engaged greater attention than even the formulation of the code of moral precepts, which incidentally is not even mentioned at this stage. There is no doubt that in maintaining the vigour and vitality of the Saṅgha, whether of the Bhikkhus or of the Bhikkhunīs, the code of the Pātimokkha played a vital part. But it seems to be equally true to say that in bringing the newly inaugurated Bhikkhunī Saṅgha into a healthy relationship with the older institution of the Bhikkhu Saṅgha, the *aṭṭhagarudhammā* were calculated to play a greater role. They take no note of moral considerations. A perfect functioning of the latter, in the case of the Bhikkhunīs too, was apparently taken for granted at this early stage of their Sāsana. That a similar state of affairs did exist even in the Bhikkhu Saṅgha in its early history is evident in the Kakacūpama Sutta, (MN. I,124).

On a closer examination of the *aṭṭhagarudhammā* we are led to make the following observations: According to these the Bhikkhu Saṅgha is looked upon as the more mature and responsible body, evidently on account of its seniority, which is capable of leading the way for the Bhikkhunī Saṅgha. This is clearly evident from the *garudhammas* 2 and 3 (Vin.II, 255). The Bhikkhunīs are expected to recognise the spiritual leadership of the Order of Bhikkhus. At least at the outset, the Bhikkhunīs had to seek the assistance of the Bhikkhus in such vital monastic rituals like the *Pātimokkhuddesa* and *Bhikkhunovāda*.

But it is also evident that, as circumstances necessitated and experience proved opportune, the Buddha did transfer some of these powers to the Bhikkhunīs themselves (ibid.259). However, the recognition of the leadership of the monks over the community of nuns and this position of the Bhikkhus *in loco parentis* to the Bhikkhunīs seem to have continued much longer. Even when the authority to recite the Pātimokkha by themselves was finally transferred to the Bhikkhunīs, the Bhikkhus were still left with the right to instruct them on its proper performance (*Anujānāmi bhikkhave bhikkhūhi bhikkhunīnaṃ ācikkhitumm̧ evaṃ pātimokkhaṃ uddiseyyāthā'ti*: Vin.II,259).

There is also evidence of a similar reservation of power in the transference of authority to the Bhikkhunīs to impose penalties and punishments on their fellow members. The Bhikkhus who carried out these acts at the outset are latterly barred from doing so and are authorised only to explain to the Bhikkhunis the proper procedure: (*Anujānāmi bhikkhave bhikkhūhi bhikkhunīnaṃ ācikkhituṃ evaṃ kammaṃ kareyyāthā'ti*: Vin.II,260). In the matter of *bhikkhunovāda* too, it was a Bhikkhu who was appointed to remind the Bhikkhunīs regularly of the proper observance of the *aṭṭhagarudhammā:* (Vin.IV,51f.).

Thus on account of this complete dependence of a Bhikkhunī on the leadership of a Bhikkhu the second of these eight *garudhammā* forbade the Bhikkhunīs from going into residence for the rains-retreat in a place where there were no Bhikkhus. The third *garudhamma* too, implies the reliance of the Bhikkhunīs on the Order of Bhikkhus in the performance of the two functions of *uposathapucchaka* and *ovadupasankamana*. Both the Bhikkhus and the Bhikkhunīs seem to have been vigilant about the proper observance of these functions which they considered, no doubt, to be vital for the healthy progress of the newly established Order of nuns. At the first sign of slackness with regard to these there is a storm of protests and we notice that the authorities take immediate action to remedy it.

These considerations are brought within the legal framework of the Bhikkhunī Sāsana and the failure to observe these come to be declared punishable offences (Ibid. 313, 315. See Bhikkhunī Pācittiya 56, 59). In other words they become part of the Bhikkhunī Pātimokkha. In the study of the *sikkhāpadas* of the Bhikkhu Pātimokkha we have already noted this interesting phenomenon of the change-over into legal statutes of what was once observed as honoured conventions.

The *garudhammā* 4, 5 and 6 concern themselves with some of the other major items of administration in the Buddhist monastic community, *viz*:(i) the performance of the *pavāraṇā* at the end of the rains retreat, (ii) the imposition of necessary penalties on the commission of a grave offence, and (iii) the conferment of *upasampadā* or higher monastic status. As far as the Bhikkhunīs are concerned, they are barred under these *garudhammā* from performing any of these acts within their own Order of the Bhikkhunī Saṅgha. These acts of the Bhikkhunīs are not considered valid unless they are carried out jointly together with the monks. However, practical considerations soon necessitated amendments to these and we see in the revised version of these conditions the sanction given to the Bhikkhunīs to perform these acts, in the first instance, by themselves. Then they are expected to bring their decisions before the Bhikkhu Saṅgha for ratification.

The following is the amended procedure for the conferment of *upasampadā* on a Bhikkhunī by the Bhikkhu Saṅgha: *Anujānāmi bhikkhave ekato upasampannāya bhikkhunīsaṅghe visuddhāya bhikkhusaṅghe upasampadan'ti:* (Vin.II. 271, 274). It shows that the candidate had been already approved by the Bhikkhunī Saṅgha. The Bhikkhunīs were also allowed to perform their *pavāraṇa* in two stages before the two assemblies. First among themselves and then before the Bhikkhu Saṅgha: (*Anujānāmi bhikkhave ajjatanā pavāretvā aparajju bhikkhusaṅghe pavāretuṃ ti*: Ibid. 275).

Thus, from the manner in which the Buddha directed the activities of the Bhikkhunīs, it becomes clear that he did realise that as the Bhikkhunīs formed a part of the single body of the Saṅgha, their decisions would affect not only themselves, but also the rest of that vast organization. Hence the Bhikkhus were given the right to advise and assist the Bhikkhunīs in their affairs, and thus regulate the destinies of the Sāsana. Public opinion must have played a considerable part in bringing Bhikkhunīs under the wing of the Bhikkhu Saṅgha. At any rate, it appears to have been considered wise to have all the important monastic activities of the Bhikkhunīs linked up with the more established and senior group of the Bhikkhu Saṅgha. However, when and wherever this advisory role had to be transferred from the collective organization of the Bhikkhu Saṅgha to a single individual, the Buddha took every necessary precaution to avoid possible abuse of privilege.

He has laid down a very comprehensive list of eight requirements which should be satisfied before a monk could be selected to the role of a *bhikkhunovādaka* to give counsel to the congregation of nuns. There seems to be little doubt about his anxiety and his foresight regarding the safety and well-being of the female members of his Order. A monk who is entrusted to preside over their welfare should conform to perfect standards of moral virtue. He should also possess a thorough knowledge of the teaching of the Master and know well the complete code of the Pāṭimokkha covering both the Bhikkhus and the Bhikkhunīs. He should be of pleasant disposition, mature in years and acceptable to the Bhikkhunīs, and above all, should in no way have been involved in a serious offence with Bhikkhunīs: (Vin. IV,51).

The three remaining *garudhammā* 1, 7 and 8, appear to have baffled some students of Buddhism as being contrary to the Buddha's general attitude to women. However, if these are examined carefully in their context, this apparent contradiction becomes less glaring. They all strive to see that the Bhikkhunīs do not, under any circumstance, assert their superiority over the Bhikkhus. We notice that even in the observance of *sikkhāpadas*, the Bhikkhunīs are to follow the lead of the Bhikkhus wherever the *sikkhāpadas* are common to both groups. The Buddha advises the Bhikkhunīs to follow the Bhikkhus in the practice of such *sikkhāpada* (*...yathā bhikkhū sikkhanti tathā tesu sikkhāpadesu sikkhathā'ti:* Vin.II, 258). But referring to the *sikkhāpada* which are peculiar to the Bhikkhunīs, he suggests that they should be followed, as they are laid down according to the letter of the law (*...yathāpaññattesu sikkhāpadesu sikkhathā'ti.* Ibid. 258).

What seems to follow from these words of instruction to the Bhikkhunīs is that even if there was a difference between the text of the *sikkhāpada* laid down for the Bhikkhus and their practice at the time, the Buddha did not think it wise, for purposes of communal harmony, to leave room for the Bhikkhunīs to be critical of this discrepancy. Such a challenge would have completely undermined the prestige and the authority of the older institution of the Saṅgha, quite out of proportion to any degree of moral good it could bring about by the correction of Bhikkhus by the Bhikkhunīs.

There is evidence to show that the Buddha was always concerned with the esteem in which the public held his monastic organization. Such a consideration was vital for its existence and prosperity. The first remarks which he made to his erring disciples as he criticised their conduct always pertains to this (*N'etam mogha purisa appasannānaṃ vā pasādāya pasannānaṃ vā bhiyyobhāvāya:* Vin.I,58; II,2; III,21,45). As much as the Buddha wanted his disciples to correct their mistakes and be of faultless conduct he did not want any of them to divulge to any one other than a Bhikkhu or a Bhikkhunī the more serious offences of their fellow members. Such an intimation was allowed only with the approval of the Bhikkhus (*Yo pana bhikkhu bhikkhussa dutthullaṃ āpattiṃ anupasampannassa āroceyya aññatra bhikkhusammutiyā pācittiyaṃ:* Vin. IV, 31.). One who violates this injunction is guilty of a Pācittiya offence (Pāc.9).

This provision was undoubtedly made with the best of intentions and should not be misjudged as contributing in any way to the perpetuation of monastic offences. On the other hand, it is in fact repeatedly declared that it is irregular for a monk to conceal intentionally an offence of one member from the rest of the community. Pācittiya 64 of the monks and Pārājikā 2 and Saṅghādisesa 9 of the nuns are all calculated to avoid such a possibility (Vin.IV,127, 216, 239). All these precautions, therefore, seem to be a part of a system of internal security set up by the Buddha in the interest of the monastic organization. They emphasise the Buddha's concern both for the public esteem and for the moral soundness of his Order.

There seems to be a general agreement about the fact that the eight *garudhammā* were laid down by the Buddha as a condition governing the establishment of the Bhikkhunī Sāsana. However, strange as it may seem, after the Bhikkhunī Sāsana was instituted under the leadership of Gotamī, she appears before Ānanda to make the request that the Buddha should remove the first *garudhamma* and allow Bhikkhus and Bhikkhunīs to pay courtesies to each other according to seniority alone (Ibid.257-58). This is hardly true to the spirit in which Gotamī accepted the *garudhammā* (Ibid.255-56.) We are inclined to think that she was here undoubtedly subjected to the pressure of her own group.

This dissentient note which we find recorded in the Cullavagga does not seem to have found general acceptance elsewhere. Of the Chinese Vinaya texts it is only the Mahīsāsakas who record it and that too with a different emphasis (*Taisho*, Vol.22, p.186 A). According to their text Gotamī, prior to her being ordained, sends Ānanda to the Buddha to request him to make this change. The Buddha refuses to do so and says that since he has now allowed women to enter the Order they should follow what has been laid down and not go against it. In the Cullavagga too, the Buddha declines to make this concession. But in trying to give a reason for this attitude of the Buddha the Theriya tradition attempts to make out that in the organization of the Sāsana social considerations, as much as moral and ethical values, loomed large in the mind of the Master. In the Cullavagga he is reported as saying: 'Not even the Titthiyas who propound imperfect doctrines sanction such homage of men towards women. How could the Tathāgata do so?' (Vin. II,258).

We should also here consider the fact that any concession for the abrogation of what had already been laid down after careful deliberation would be grossly contradictory to the ideal which the Buddha and his early disciples appear to have upheld regarding the observance of the rules and regulations laid down for the guidance of monastic life (Ibid.III,231). The reply which the Buddha seems to have given to Gotamī in the Chinese version of the Mahīsāsaka Vinaya is definitely more in keeping with this spirit. But we should take note of the fact that this reply would run contrary to the Theriya tradition, which at some stage,seems to have accommodated the idea that the Buddha conceded the abrogation of the minor rules (D.II,14 & VIn. II,287).

As far as we are aware there is one other Vinaya tradition which records a challenge of the *garudhammā.* The Chinese version of the Dharmagupta Vinaya has a chapter entitled Bhikkhunī Khandhaka wherein the question is asked whether the Bhikkhunīs cannot accuse the Bhikkhus under any circumstances (*Taisho*,Vol.22, p.927 A). The Buddha replies to say that they could not do so even if the Bhikkhus violated the rules of discipline or were guilty of offences. These two protests on the part of the Bhikkhunīs seem to show that the Bhikkhunī Saṅgha, or at least a section of it, resisted what it considered to be harsh legislation unfavourable to them.

At the same time one has to view dispassionately the position of the Buddha, who as the head of the Bhikkhu Saṅgha which was already a well-groomed institution, had to safeguard against its disintegration through dispute and discontent. The fifth accusation levelled against Ānanda at the First Council, that he agitated for the admission of women into the Order (Vin.II,289), is a clear indication that even after the recognised success of the Bhikkhunī Sāsana (Apadāna II,535;V,79) there was a section of the Bhikkhus who formed as it were a consolidated opposition against it. The motive for such an attitude could have been generated by the fear of being eclipsed by the newer Order.

The Chinese version of the Mahīsāsaka Vinaya includes a statement which is ascribed to the Buddha which seems to lend support to this assumption. The Buddha says that if there were no Bhikkhunīs in the Sāsana, then after his death the male and female lay-devotees (*upāsaka* and *upāsikās*) would have honoured the Bhikkhus in diverse ways. But now that the Bhikkhunīs had entered the Order it would not happen so (*Taisho,* Vol.22, p.186 B). It is difficult here to decide how and why the presence of Bhikkhunīs in the Sāsana brought about such a radical change in the attitude of laymen towards the Bhikkhus.

Why were the Bhikkhus deprived of the honour that would have been theirs had not the Bhikkhunīs appeared on the scene? Are the Bhikkhunīs to be held responsible for the loss of prestige of the Bhikkhus? At any rate, this record of the Mahīsāsakas was undoubtedly representative of the opinion of the day regarding the Bhikkhunī Sāsana.

The Pali records of the Theriya tradition which belong to an earlier phase of the history of the Sāsana give expression to a similar feeling in the chastisement of Ānanda in whom ultimately lay the responsibility for the admission of women into the Order. An echo of this is felt in the Mahīsāsaka Vinaya where Ānanda apologises to the Buddha for having requested him to permit women to enter the Order. But the Buddha absolves him saying that he did so unwittingly under the influence of Māra (*Taisho,* Vol.22, p.186 A). The Theriya tradition is not alone again in expressing the fact that the presence of women in the Sāsana would reduce its life span by half. We find it recorded in the Chinese version of the Dharmagupta Vinaya that the Buddha told Ānanda that if women did not enter the Order it would have lasted 500 years longer (Ibid.p.923 C. See also Vin.II,256).

It becomes clear from what has been said so far that at the time of crystalization of Theriya traditions two ideas regarding the establishment of the Bhikkhunī Sāsana stood out clearly. A section of the Bhikkhu Saṅgha was reproachful of Ānanda because he interceded with the Buddha for the sake of the Bhikkhunīs. The admission of women was also considered a categorical danger to the successful continuance of the Sāsana. In the light of all this evidence a study of the *garudhammā* reveals to us the fact that the Buddha was keenly conscious of the need to steer clear of the possible rivalries of the Bhikkhus and the Bhikkhunīs and maintain healthy and harmonious relations between the two groups.

The Human Resource

as viewed from the Buddhist religio - cultural angle

More than ever before it has now become vital that policy-makers at all levels become sensitive to the need of value judgements. It is then and only then that they can, with a fair measure of conviction, face the consequences of their decisions and hold themselves responsible for same. We often undertake to do many things, but often with very little qualitative assesment of what we are doing and with even less thought as for whose benefit we are doing them.

With these prefatory remarks now let me present my paper to you. It must be stated in no uncertain terms at the very outset that a major theme in Buddhist social philosophy is the successful harnessing of the manpower resources of a country. One must carefully examine the target which the Buddhists mean to achieve thereby and the methods they propose to adopt to make such a venture a success.

In order to analyse, assess and administer manpower resources available to us, I should first explain the Buddhist concept of man as a prelude to our discussion. Man is said to be man, according to Buddhism, because of his mental accomplishment: *manassa ussannattā manussā. Mana* means 'mind' and *ussannatta* means 'the lofty heights it has reached.' Let us examine this a little further. Man, unlike the animal, does not move on in life through built-in responses.

Man is gifted with the capacity to make decisions, adjust himself to new situations, be sensitive not only to his own feelings but slso to those of others, make concessions and sacrifices on what are carefully judged by him to be valid considerations. Man, according to Buddhism, is such a functionally effective and efficient unit in the social machinery of the human community. He is not subordinated to a higher will above himself. What he does is not dictated by a higher authority above and beyond humanity. He works on a basically horizontal, humanistic value system which invariably forms also the basis of his transcendental aspirations.

According to correct Buddhist thinking one has to start with what is known and near and make that the basis for everything that is beyond and is hoped for. It is in this sense that we would make bold to say that the road to Nirvāṇa runs through the highways of society. Here one cannot fail to respect the position that the social philosophy of Buddhism prepares the ground-plan for its religious super-structure. It is equally true that a Buddhist cannot expect to reach his religious goal without a sound social philosophy.

Now let me start with the first propostition of Buddhist social philosophy, namely the *pañcasīla* or the Code of Five Moral Precepts. It is not unusual to hear occasional rumblings from our midst, from all manner of pepole, about the difficulty of observing these simple basic injunctions which are rooted in an awareness of fundamental human rights. A clear and unconfused knowledge of basic Buddhist teachings would reveal to anyone the intense degree of social concern and social relevance they embody. They uphold a person's right for the safety of his life and a person's right over his possessions. These are universally acclaimed human rights.

Here I wish to draw your attention to the U.N. charter on Fundamental Human Rights. They do not demand anybody's leanings to a particular religious faith or to a particular political creed. They can very well be practised and upheld without any thoughts of religious conversion. This universality is further attested in Buddhist texts where the *pañcasīla* becomes the basic admonition of the Universal Monarch or Rājā Cakkavatti who has to be accepted by the whole world as their one and only ruler. The ruler, in turn, tells the people that his major concern is that the world should respect the moral order, and that he does not interfere with the basic rights of people. As long as the moral order is maintained in a manner that serves mankind, it is not the intention of the Cakkavatti to interfere with the political structure of any country. In any country where Buddhism has contributed to the formation of the cultural milieu, one has to take serious notice of the above remarks about the insistence on the moral order before attempting to examine or analyse the socio-economic problems of that country.

I shall now introduce to you in brief some of the authentic Buddhist texts which deal with the subject of manpower resources directly and precisely in terms of social requirements.

Kūṭadanta Sutta of the Digha Nikaya (DN.1,135ff.) handles this at the state level on the basis of professional skills and personal aptitude and temperament with a view to ensuring maximum utilization of manpower resources. Strict adherence to casting the right type in the right place is recommended. Further it is also recognized that there should be adequate stimuli and inspiration from the employer for the maximum output of work from the employee. Satisfactory provision of food at work place, adequate remuneration for the work done and further aids like health care and medical attention for the successful pursuance of the employment undertaken are among the interesting issues dealt with in the above quoted sutta.

On the other hand the Sigāla Sutta (DN.III,180f.) deals with this issue of utilization of manpower resources in the community from the domestic angle, i.e. at the familial level. The main theme there is the respectful recognition of the services rendered, and in this case, particularly to the family as a unit. The relationships discussed there imply familial, extra-familial and inter-familial considerations. While the family is recognized as the basic unit of social operation the satisfactory administration of the family appears to have also regarded as important the services rendered by many others from different areas of service like the teacher (*ācariya*) who contributes to the education of the children in the home and the religious men (*samaṇabrāhmaṇa*) who provide the moral and spiritual leadership to the entire family while standing, as it were, outside the pale of the family proper (Ibid.).

In the Sigāla Sutta, further to this recognition of the services rendered, there are virtually detailed codes of conduct which determine the relationship in which one party stands to the other. The relationship is respectfully reciprocal and does not make one subservient to another. As in the Kūṭadanta Sutta, in the Sigāla Sutta too, stimulative measures are further recommended, thus building up a healthy morale within the work-community, not only in those directly employed but also in those conected with the workmen in diverse relationships such as a workman's spouse and offspring.

By now it should be clear to us that a point which is reiterated in Buddhist teachings is that man must hold man in complete respect, that being the very spirit of the concept of *mettā* or *maitrī*, i.e. unbounded love or loving-kindness. It also implies that no one should do anything that jeopardises the interests of the other, (*parabyābādhāya saṃvatteyya:* MN. I, 416 Ambalaṭṭhikā Rāhulovāda Sutta), that he must not deprive another of what legitimately belongs to him (*...parassa paravittūpakaraṇaṃ* ...MN. I, 287). For it is indicated that a man's possesssions form the basis of his happiness (*Paravittūpakaraṇaṃ'ti tass'eva parassa vittūpakaraṇaṃ tuṭṭhijananaṃ parikkhārabhaṇḍakaṃ* at M.A.11. 329: Commentary to the Sāleyyaka Sutta; MN.I,285 f).

Let me now elaborate for your benefit some of the theses formulated by the Buddhists on this issue. Utilization of manpower resources immediately implies employment of some sort, either by an employer or as self-employment. An employer comes in two categories, either as state or private sector. Leaving self-employment to be organized and stabilized through self-regulation, the question of employer - employee relationships where two groups or individuals are involved are thoroughly dealt with in these Buddhist sources. They had several major reasons for taking upon themselves this task. A well-regulated system of human relationships was deemed necessary at all levels for social harmony, peace and prosperity.

On the side of economic development where greater productivity resulting from efficient administration of work was necessary, it was vital that every unit of the working community was smoothly integrated. This, it was realised on the other hand, was possible only where people derived the maximum or at least the optimum happiness in life that they choose to enjoy. This is what makes them happy and comfortable. Buddhist texts use two valuable words in these contexts, namely *sukheti* - comforts and *pīṇeti* - pleases or satisfies. As we now examine the Buddhist stand with regard to employer- employee relationships we will discover how much these two concepts loom large in the minds of those who formulated the policies. The policies as laid down in the Kūṭadanta Sutta quoted above embrace three major areas. There are:

1. Job- satisfaction for the employee and the maximum utilization of skills and aptitudes from the point of view of the employer.
2. Adequate remuneration for work done and recognition of service rendered.
3. Sensitivity to the physical and emotional needs of the employee.

Under the consideration of job satisfaction the Kūṭadanta Sutta which envisages the State as the employer notes that people should be employed according to competence and aptitude. Several avenues of employment like agriculture, trade, public administration are mentioned and the assignment and appointment is to be according to each one's choice, literally in the avenue in which they persevere or are competent in: *ussahati*. Contentment among the employees and consequent productivity in the work sector is envisaged. As further stimuli to this it is suggested that all workmen (excepting those engaged in trade in this context) are to be provided with meals daily (*devasikaṃ bhattaṃ*) at their work place in addition to their regular monthly wages (*māsikaṃ paribbayaṃ*).

This was a must and had to be arranged to suit the workers' convenience. It had to be more than a mere frugal meal. Special meals or delicacies had to be even occassionally introduced. Literary evidence shows that this was no mere injunction confined to the theoretical tradition of the books. In the Mahāvaṃsa (Mhv. Ch.50, *vv*.18-21) it is stated that during the construction of the Mahāthūpa at Anuradhapura, i.e. Ruvanvelisaya, King Duṭu Gemunu (Duṭṭha Gāmaṇī) provided four canteens at the four gates for the benefit of the workmen which carried in their stocks, in addition to items of food and drink, "many garments, different ornaments, fragrant flowers, sugar as well as the five perfumes for the mouth." Mark well the King's wish, while providing these facilities: "Let them take of these as they will when they have laboured as they will." Observing this command the King's work-people alloted (the wages).

Quite unwittingly, while commenting on Duṭu Gemunu's policy, we have now come to the second point indicated above, viz. adequate remuneration or wages. Before proceeding further let me stress here again that the provision of food for workmen is in addition to the regular wages. The word used is *bhatta* and *vetana* (*bhatta* = food, *vetana* = wages).

This is the sense in which it is used in the early Buddhist texts, in the historical tradition associated with Duṭu Gemunu and in the

Commentaries of Venerable Buddhaghosa. But it is unfortunate that the intellectual giants of Sri Lanka of more recent years have slipped off their pedestals and interpreted this as wages for food (Sinhala: *bat sandahā vāṭup*). This tended to take away from the mind of the employer his obligation to provide food for his workmen and from the employee the basis for a legitimate demand which was supported by the cultural tradition of the land. What a national calamity and what a breach in the growth of a healthy socialist outlook.

Let us now proceed to examine our last item on the list, i.e. the employer's sensitivity to the physical and emotional needs of the employee. It is indicated as a first requirement that work should be allocated, keeping in mind the physical fitness and capacity of the workmen, lighter work being given to women and juvenile workers. Medical care in case of illness is specifically mentioned. On the emotional side several specific items mentioned reveal the need on the part of the employer to win the goodwill of his employees. Luxury items of food like delicacies are to be offered to workers from time to time. Provision is also to be made to make gifts of clothing and ornaments during festive seasons, in addition to the bonuses paid regularly on this account. Thus a vast fund of goodwill is being built which not only sustains without any interruption the ventures undertaken by the employer, State or otherwise, but also nurtures such a vital spirit of comradeship between the two groups completely eliminating noisy slogans about exploitation.

Speaking of just uses of wealth (*bhogānaṃ ādiyā*), Buddhist texts make special mention of the contribution an employer makes to elevate the quality of life of his workmen and to give them the optimum happiness they expect as an integral part of decent living. (*sukhenti, pīṇenti*) in recognition of the service they have rendered to him in the production of his wealth. The Aṅguttara Nikāya (AN.III,77 and also 45) in a very comprehensive survey of money and its meaningful use (*bhogānaṃ ādiyā*) referred to above, mentions both those employed at domestic level (*dāsa-kammakāra-porisā*) as well as those in larger agricultural and industrial concerns (*khetta-kammanta-sāmanta-samvohāra*).

Finally, one glance at the Sigāla Sutta (DN.III,180-194). This is essentially a code of layman's ethics for social harmony, domestic happiness and economic well-being. The heights of culture to which it can elevate a man of any society is not at all adequately appreciated. That it speaks in no uncertain terms of regulated hours of work and overtime payment is hardly known. In the process of translation its treasures are buried under the earth brought up in the process of digging (See: Dialogues of the Buddha - Rhys Davids, Vol.III, p.182). This sutta which calls upon the householder to put the house in order under one family unit, extends this process of regularization, linking one family with another, thus having no single individual in the community who is not related to the entire community in some definite wholesome way. Through this process every one is respected, generously and genuinely, for the service rendered in the interest of the human community. It is for this reason that the sutta is called the Salutation to all Directions: *disā namassana*.

Thus, in the teachings of the Buddha, delivered to the world more than two and a half millennia ago, one discovers a wealth of information which can be utilized to guide the destinies of man, without any foreign aid from above or below, through a sheer policy of human magnanimity and humanitarian considerations evolved through honesty and love.

Death

Let it be thy guide through life

I do not wish to be deemed paradoxical if I said that death, or more precisely awareness of death, guards life and provides in turn a ceaseless source of inspiration. It is with this awareness that Buddhism waxes eloquent while it is on the theme of death (*maraṇānussati* or contemplation on death).

Man is born with death in his hands (*maraṇantaṃ hi jīvitaṃ*). Death of man does not lie in the hands of another, beyond his world of existence. If one does enter into a contract with another power regarding the early or late arrival of death, then one has to be continuously supplicating for its deferment. For if one had the choice, there is not the slightest doubt that every one would reject death and opt for life.

Death is real. It is part of life and is built into it as part and parcel of the physiological process of living. Death is a characteristic failure of what is called life. We do not need to arbitrarily give an explanation for its occurrence. It makes little sense to keep life in the hands of one and leave death in the hands of another. Well before the moon-shuttle thirteen attempts failed to make its journey to its destination. The men at NASA knew of the possibility of such an eventuality. Every one cooperating in the production of these space shuttles were warned about this situation and were called upon to strive towards the elimination of all such possible defects. It is this awareness and anticipation which enabled the men on earth who knew what they were doing to bring back the ailing space ship 13 safely to earth.

It is for a very similar reason that the Buddhist believes that being armed with a good and sound philosophy of death is to win half the battle of life. Death's reality and bitterness being what it is, men and women of all ages, at all times and everywhere, who have not been able to adequately forewarn themselves about it, are seen lying paralyzed with shock and grief when it has fatally stung those near and dear to them.

The Buddhist story of Paṭācārā and her first-born dead infant, with its vibrantly comforting enunciation of the reality of death, as propounded by Paṭācārā herself to the grieving five hundred mothers (*pañcasatā paṭācārā)* who came seeking her for a word of comfort (See Therīgāthā *vv.* 127 ff.) should be a lesson to all mankind for all times. She says: " These children come to us, from whither we know not. They leave us with no intimation to us. While they are with us, we appropriate them as our own. On their departure, we grieve over their loss... As he came, so has he gone. What lamentation could be there? "

Yassa maggaü na jānāsi āgatassa gatassa vā
taṃ kuto āgataṃ puttaṃ mama putto'ti rodasi.
....
yathāgato tathāgato kā tattha paridevanā?

Thig.*vv.*127-130.

The Dhammapadaṭṭhakathā (DhpA. I, 260-275 and DhpA.III, 432 f.), perhaps due to a deviant tradition derived from the Apadāna, which has also at the same time influenced the Commentarial tradition of the Therīgāthā Aṭṭhakathā, interchanges these two stories of Paṭācārā and Kisāgotamī and transfers this story of the dead son to Kisāgotamī, with the very dramatic story of the Buddha asking her to get some mustard seeds from a home where no death had ever occurred. What Kisāgotamī apparently sought from the Buddha was some medication (*bhesajjaṃ*) for the restoration to life of her dead child. But the Buddha, instead of making a blunt refusal to do so and turning away this grieving mother, wisely used this strategy. It was more profound a lesson to teach and to learn that there never was and never shall be a home in which no death has ever occurred than to perform a miracle through divine power whereby a single mortal son is raised from the dead.

The Therīgāthā makes no mention of any mustard seed story, neither with regard to Kisāgotamī nor Paṭācārā. But the Therīgāthā Commentary to Kisāgotami's verses, quoting the Apadāna (ThigA. p. 181), reveals the origin of this story:

Tadā ekena sandiṭṭhā upetvābhi Sakkuttamaṃ
avocaṃ dehi bhesajjaṃ puttasañjīvakan'ti bho.
" Na vijjante matā yasmiṃ gehe siddhatthakaṃ tato
āharā" ti jino āha vinayopāya-kovido.
Tadā gamitvā Sāvatthiṃ na labhiṃ tādisaṃ gharaṃ
kuto siddhatthakaṃ tasmā tato laddhā satiṃ ahaṃ.
Kuṇapaṃ chaḍḍayitvāna upesiṃ lokanāyakaṃ.

vv. 23-26

Two important items of information emerge from this. 1. This story of the mustard seeds goes back to the Apadāna as its primary source. 2. This Apadāna tradition also introduces the more or less Mahāyāna idea of *upāya-kausalya* or maganimous strataegy ascribed to the Buddha, referred to here as *vinayopāya-kovido.*

This self-same Dhammapadaṭṭhakathā makes Paṭācārā play Kisāgotamī's role of being the victim of the sixfold tragedy. But according to the Therīgāthā, it is Kisāgotamī and not Paṭācārā who is the victim of this intense multiple tragedy of losing her two infant children, her huband, her mother and father and her brother, all on one single occasion. Kisāgotamī in the Therīgāthā speaks of it as the tragedy of her own life. See Therīgāthā *vv.* 219 -223 where she speaks of the death of her two sons and her husband etc:

Dve me puttā kālakatā patī ca panthe mato kapaṇikāya
mātā pitā ca bhātā ca ḍayhanti ekacitakāyaṃ.

v. 219

Ahaṃ amhi kantasallā ohitabhārā kataṃ me karaṇīyaṃ
Kisāgotamī therī suvimuttacittā imaṃ bhaṇī'ti.

v. 223

It is also important to note that the above verse 219 of the Therīgāthā appears in a slightly different form in the Dhammapadaṭṭhakathā as

Ubho puttā kālakatā pante mayhaṃ patī mato
mātā pitā ca bhātā ca ekacitakasmiṃ ḍayhare.

(DhpA. I, 266).

This is the version preserved in the Apadāna (Ap. p.115) to which our Therīgathā Commentary seems to be very much indebted.

With or without this confusion in the identification of Paṭācārā (Thig. *vv.* 112-121 and 127-132) and Kisāgotamī (Thig. *vv.* 213-223), these two hapless women, together with Vāseṭṭhī (Thig. *vv.* 133-138), show the world the very blessings of the Buddha's appearance in their midst, although he evidently never lifted a finger to raise their children from death. To them, as well as to all mankind, it was an all-time triumph over death. That is why we have in the wake of Paṭācārā's spiritual gain, as mentioned in the Therīgāthā, a first batch of thirty grieving mothers and after that yet another five hundred, more or less, reach the same heights that Paṭācārā herself reached. These are the lessons with a universal message of which the world has all the time a need to learn.

The pain one suffers in the process of living, one must not expect to deaden or obliterate by injecting the cocaine of divine intervention. Of this, the Buddha was specific and forthright. The awareness of this gives human life a new and courageous sense of direction, both in the process of living here right now, and in higher aspirations of spiritual uplift.

One must here recollect how the young monk Raṭṭhapāla clarified to King Koravya, the ruler of the land of Kurus (See MN. II, 68), the true Buddhist world-view that man has no refuge (*attāṇo loko*), besides himself, to which he can go seeking succour or shelter. And also that there is no super-power (*anabhissaro*) who guides and presides over the destiny of man.

Death versus Life

Now let us take a closer look at the concepts of life and death in Buddhism. Taking as an example a long cinematographic film reel which consists of hundreds of single frames, the life of man on earth as known to us could be equated to any one of those frames. Isolating any one of them for a closer scrutiny does not entitle us to forget the rest which may be located both before and after it.

Buddhism handles the life of man with this total vision. Proof for the reality of this comes to us not only from the Buddha who is both the Enlightened One and our guide. "Through countless lives I did roam" (*Anekajātisaṃsāraṃ sandhāvissaṃ anibbisaṃ*), he says. His disciples who have accepted his teaching, and have lived to perfection the life he has indicated, are themselves capable of assuring us of the truth of this, by telling us of their former births and the experiences there in those existences.

Here is Gotama Thera (Thag. *vv.* 258-260) who recounts for us his experience in former lives.

In my journeying through *saṃsāra*
To burning hells I went.
And to the world
Of hungry ghosts, again and again.
Among animals who suffer immense pain,
Many a time was I born in the past.
I did enjoy life among humans.
So it was for me in the heavenly worlds.
I have fully comprehended that
All existences which are conditioned states
Are essenceless and are far too turbulent.
Not for me then are *saṃsāric* existences.
Mindfully have I now attained peace.

(Translated by the author).

Therī Sumedhā is equally eloquent in her utterances in the Therīgāthā (Thig. *vv.* 454-456). Thus she says:

They who love to roll on in *saṃsāra,*
Seeking birth in the heavenly worlds,
They know not the truths proclaimed by the Buddha.
Being in the transient realm of things,
Even birth amidst the devas is of no worth.
They are foolish indeed who dread not
At being born again and again.
In the four lower states, or in the two above,
Beings get their births somehow.
In the lower decadent states, one never gets
The chance of renouncing the word.

(Translated by the author).

This stretching of life through time and space is the basic Buddhist doctrine of *saṃsāra*. The fact that all beings inherit this continuity of life is what the Buddhist texts teach us as *bhava* or becoming. The dynamism of that process is what is implied in the term *saṃsāra*: *sandhāvati saṃsarati,* which is said of the life process of a being in *saṃsāra*, that he runs along or rolls on.

What is connoted by both terms *bhava* and *saṃsāra* can be equated to the length and continuity of the film reel to which we referred above. In *bhava* or *saṃsāra*, the appearance or manifestation of an individual results in *jāti* or birth, and the span of life from birth to death is the equivalent of a single frame of that film reel.

Let us now ask ourselves as to what sets this life process in motion. What determines the very nature of our life here and what pushes us on from one existence to another, to a vastness of incalculable time and space?. Thus the staggering allusion to *saṃsāra* as *anamataggo ayaṃ bhikkhave saṃsāro*: "O monks, infinitely extensive is this life process called *saṃsāra*." It is primarily *kamma* or our own activities in which we get engaged and involved in the process of living. Such *kamma* is generated through our own weaknesses on account of which we get attracted to or repelled by the world around us. But life certainly is possible without these excesses in either direction.

Heedful of Destruction

We must be mindful of our needs which arise in the process of living and be able to satisfy them in socially and individually justifiable and agreeable ways. We must also be mindful not to err on the side of greed which results in being aggressive and anti-social in our acquisitive pursuits. We must at the same time be sensitively aware of possible egoistic eruptions on our part and guard ourselves against pushing our frontiers too far, crushing everybody and everything that comes our way. This is where our human frailty of hatred raises its ugly head, where we determine by ourselves and for ourselves what we like and what we dislike, and thereafter explosively eliminate whatever we suspect to be standing on our way. A good example of this comes to us from the time of the Buddha where King Pasenadi of Kosala is said to have had his army commander Bandhula Malla assassinated on suspicions that he was plotting against the king. It was no more than a suspicion based on mere wild allegations.

The vicious trails of greed and hatred invariably lead to calamitous reactions like jealousies and rivalries which finally end in brutal murders and assassinations at individual level and in outrageous invasions and devastating wars at collective level.

In relation to this, the Buddhist position is simply this. The Buddhist has to be heedful not only of the external destruction and damage such behaviour causes to others besides himself but also of the internal and psychical deterioration which such violent behaviour sets in motion within himself. This, the Buddhist calls *akusala* or *pāpa*, i.e. evil or sinful behaviour which is self-damaging. Such behaviour is damaging both to life here and life beyond.

The Buddhist's awareness of death is educative. He is made to reckon with the fact that while life in the world, with a multiplicity of pleasure-yielding relationships, is one that one would wish for, at the same time, any single instance of death in that complex, like the sword of Democles, is an immensely painful reality. With this truth staring in the face, the Buddhist must make a more sane and sound reckoning of life. This is the Buddhist search for truth in life.

In the world of motoring we have now evolved to the stage of the over-drive. It makes exciting driving, in spite of dangerous corners and slippery patches. But its break-neck risks are far too many. We need to know our roads and drive with sense and judgement. So it is with life. Let death and awareness of death be thy guide through life.

THE BUDDHIST PUBLICATION SOCIETY

The BPS is an approved charity dedicated to making known the Teaching of the Buddha, which has a vital message for people of all creeds. Founded in 1958, the BPS has published a wide variety of books and booklets covering a great range of topics. Its publications include accurate annotated translations of the Buddha's discourses, standard reference works, as well as original contemporary expositions of Buddhist thought and practice. These works present Buddhism as it truly is—a dynamic force which has influenced receptive minds for the past 2500 years and is still as relevant today as it was when it first arose. A full list of our publications will be sent upon request. Write to:

The Hony. Secretary
BUDDHIST PUBLICATION SOCIETY
P.O. Box 61
54, Sangharaja Mawatha
Kandy • Sri Lanka
E–mail: bps@ids.lk/bps@metta.lk
Website: http: //www.lanka.com/dhamma

Buddhism/Asian Religions BP 420S

A Manual of the Excellent Man

Ledi Sayadaw (1846–1923) was one of the greatest Burmese Buddhist monks of the modern era, renowned throughout the Theravada Buddhist world as a scholar, writer, and meditation master. The author of more than seventy manuals, he became the "father" of the modern insight meditation tradition which spread from Myanmar outwards to the wider world. While highly learned in the Buddhist scriptures, he had the knack of writing in a lively, direct, and scintillating style, lacing his explanations of Buddhist doctrine with original and illuminating similes.

The present manual was written in response to a letter from a lay follower posing ten questions on important points of Buddhist teaching. The work begins with an explanation of the Theravada conception of the Bodhisatta, the aspirant to supreme Buddhahood, and of the ten perfections a Bodhisattsa must fulfil to reach Perfect Enlightenment. The author then launches out into a detailed exploration of the "five aggregates" that make up human existence. As his treatise unfolds he also gives coverage to the Four Noble Truths, dependent origination, the five kinds of Māras, and the nature of Nibbāna. Again and again, the Sayadaw impresses on his readers the need to take up the practice of the Dhamma in full earnestness, not remaining content with mere deeds of merit but striving along the path of insight meditation that leads to realization of the goal.

Buddhism/Asian Religions BP 402S

Rebirth as Doctrine and Experience

Francis Story (Anagārika Sugatānanda) was a British-born Buddhist who lived in Asian countries for twenty-five years, deeply studying the Buddhist philosopy of life. From the time of his early contacts with Buddhism, Story had a special interest in the subject of rebirth, which grew keener during his time in Burma, when he encountered individuals who could actually recall their previous lives. He wrote prolifically on the doctrinal side of the Buddhist rebirth teaching and on its correlate, the doctrine of karma. His interest in cases of rebirth memories finally led him to assist Dr. Ian Stevenson in tracing, investigating, and studying such cases in Sri Lanka, Thailand, and India. The present book contains Story's essays on the theme of rebirth as well as case studies that he undertook in collaboration with Professor Stevenson, the foremost American investigator of reported rebirth memories. These case studies, which make fascinating reading, lend strong evidential support to the hypothesis of rebirth and thus help to illuminate the ultimate questions concerning human destiny after death.

The Author

Ven. Dhammavihari, formerly Prof. Jotiya Dhirasekera, was ordained as a member of the Buddhist Sangha on 18th May 1990 at the age of sixty-nine. He graduated from the University of Ceylon, Colombo in 1945, majoring in Sanskrit. He thereafter taught in the Department of Pali and Buddhist Studies. In 1949 he proceeded to the Cambridge University, England where he pursued studies in Chinese, Japanese and Tibetan.

He has taught Buddhism and Pali at the University of Ceylon, Colombo (1946–1949) and Peradeniya (1952–1969). In 1964 Peradeniya University awarded him the Ph.D. degree for his thesis on Buddhist Monastic Discipline. From 1969 to 1972 he was Professor of Buddhist Studies at the University of Toronto, Canada.

Since his return to Sri Lanka in 1972, he had been the Editor-in-Chief of the Encyclopaedia of Buddhism and Director of the Postgraduate Institute of Pali and Buddhist Studies. His writings include a collection of Buddhist essays entitled **A Correct Vision** and **A Life Sublime. His** *magnum opus*, **Buddhist Monastic Discipline**, is published in the Ministry of Higher Education Research Publication Series, Sri Lanka, 1982.

He is a broadcaster and a contributor to the written and the electronic media on Buddhist subjects both at national and international levels. He has travelled widely covering Canada, U.S.A., England, Europe, Australia, New Zealand, Oman, China, Korea, Japan, Thailand, Cambodia and Myanmar.

He is presently the founder-Director of the International Buddhist Research and Information Centre (IBRIC), Sri Lanka.